It's fun to draw
Dinosaurs
and other prehistoric creatures

Mark Bergin

Author:

Mark Begin was born in Hastings, England. He has illustrated an award winning series and written over twenty books. He has done many book designs, layouts and storyboards in many styles including cartoon for numerous books, posters and adverts. He lives in Bexhill-on-sea with his wife and three children.

Editorial Assistant:
Rob Walker

HOW TO USE THIS BOOK:

Start by following the numbered splats on the left hand page. These steps will ask you to add some lines to your drawing. The new lines are always drawn in red so you can see how the drawing builds from step to step. Read the 'You can do it!' splats to learn about drawing and colouring techniques you can use.

Published in Great Britain in MMXI by
Book House, an imprint of
The Salariya Book Company Ltd
25 Marlborough Place, Brighton BN1 1UB
www.salariya.com
www.book-house.co.uk

ISBN-13: 978-1-906714-34-5

1 3 5 7 9 8 6 4 2

A CIP catalogue record for this book is available from the British Library.

Printed and bound in China.

PAPER FROM
SUSTAINABLE FORESTS

Visit our website at **www.book-house.co.uk**
or go to **www.salariya.com** for **free** electronic versions of:
You Wouldn't Want to be an Egyptian Mummy!
You Wouldn't Want to be a Roman Gladiator!
You Wouldn't Want to be a Polar Explorer!
You Wouldn't Want to Sail on a 19th-Century Whaling Ship!

Visit our Bookhouse 100 channel on Youtube to see Mark Bergin doing step by step illustrations:

www.youtube.com/user/BookHouse100

Contents

Diplodocus

Di-plod-OH-kuss

1 Start with the head.

2 Add a dot for the eye and two leaves.

3 Draw two lines for the neck.

4 Draw an oval shape for the body.

5 Draw four legs.

6 Draw two long lines for a tail.

you can do it!

Use felt-tip for the lines and colour in with crayon, using your fingers to smudge colours together.

splat-a-fact

Diplodocus had the longest tail of any animal that has ever walked on earth.

splat-a-fact

Fifteen tall men lying end to end in a line would measure the same length as a Diplodocus.

Tyrannosaurus rex

Tie-RAN-oh-sore-us

1 Draw a rectangle with a half circle.

2 Draw a smaller rectangle and another half circle.

3 Draw dots for a nose and an eye, add zig-zag lines for teeth.

4 Add lines for the body.

5 Draw in the arms and the legs.

you can do it!

Paint the Tyrannosaurus green then draw lines with a yellow wax crayon, then colour in with felt-tip or paint. The wax crayon acts as a resistant to the paint.

splat-a-fact

Tyrannosaurus rex means 'tyrant lizard king'. A large meat eater, Tyrannosaurus ate large dinosaurs like Triceratops.

Ankylosaurus

An-keel-oh-SAW-rus

1 Start with the head and eyes.

2 Add a mouth, a nostril and three spikes.

3 Draw a big oval shape for the body.

you can do it!
Use felt-tip for the lines and then add colour with watercolour paints. Use a sponge to dab on more colour for added texture.

4 Draw two lines for the tail, with small ovals at the end.

splat-a-fact
The Ankylosaurus could swing its big, bony tail to club its enemies.

5 Draw four legs.

6 Draw a line through the middle of the body.

7 Add spikes.

Pteranodon

Terr-AN-oh-don

1 Start with the head.

2 Add a tongue and a dot for the eye.

3 Draw two lines for the neck and a circle for the body.

4 Draw in the curved shape of the wings.

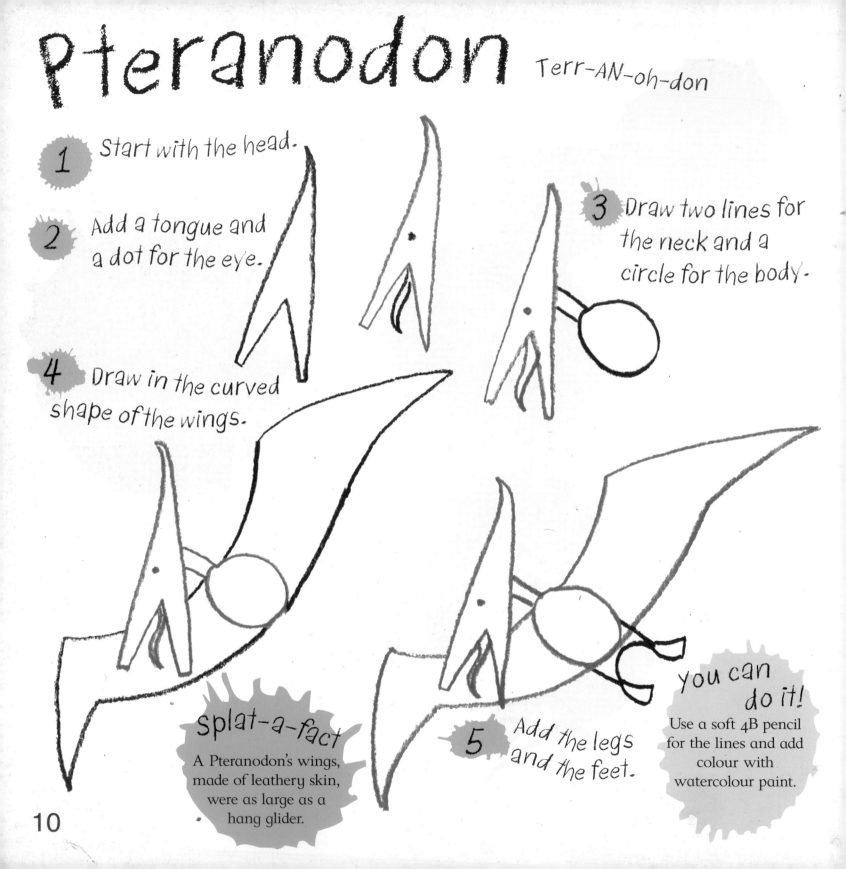

splat-a-fact

A Pteranodon's wings, made of leathery skin, were as large as a hang glider.

5 Add the legs and the feet.

you can do it!

Use a soft 4B pencil for the lines and add colour with watercolour paint.

10

Dimetrodon

Di-MET-ro-don

1 Start with the head.

2 Add the mouth, a nostril and a circle with a dot for the eye.

you can do it!

Use a felt-tip pen for the lines and then use coloured fine liners. Use straight lines, squiggly lines and cross-hatching to add interest.

5 Draw a big curved shape with straight lines in it.

3 Draw two lines for the neck, joined to a big oval.

4 Draw two lines to add the tail.

splat-a-fact

A Dimetrodon's back 'sail' was made of tough skin and long bones.

6 Add four legs.

12

13

Parasaurolophus

Para-saw-ROLL-oh-fuss

1 Start with the head with a small mouth and a dot for the eye.

2 Draw two lines for a crest and add nostrils.

3 Draw two lines for the neck, an oval shape for the body and two curved lines for the tail.

you can do it!
Paint the Parasaurolophus yellow and pink then scribble lines with a yellow wax crayon. Add colour with paint. The wax acts as a resistant to the paint.

splat-a-fact
Parasaurolophus had the biggest head crest of all the duck-billed dinosaurs.

4 Draw in two legs and two arms.

14

15

Pachycephalosaurus

pack-ee-seff-ah-low-saw-rus

1 Start with a head and an eye.

2 Add the mouth, a nostril, two nose spikes and some small circles.

3 Add two lines for the neck, a big oval, two curved lines for the tail and two arms.

Splat- a fact

A Pachycephalosaurus was the same height as a double decker bus when it stood upright to feed.

you can do it!

Use a felt-tip for the lines and add colour with chalky pastels. Use your finger to smudge the colours.

4 Add two legs with clawed feet.

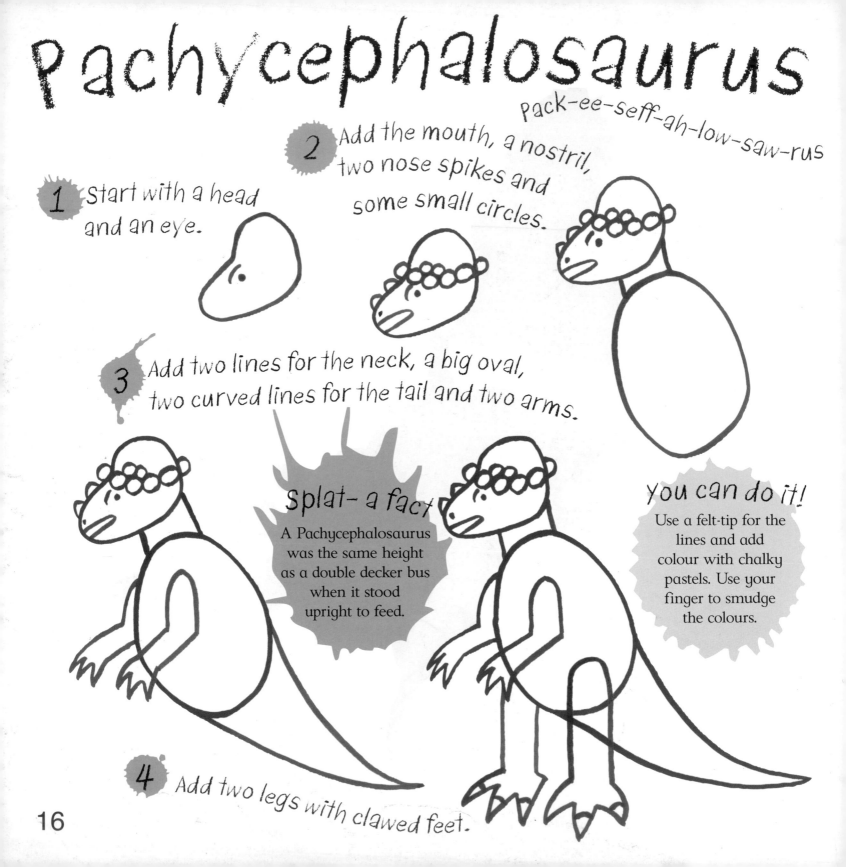

Stegosaurus

stegg-oh-SAW-rus

1 Start with the head.

2 Add the mouth and dots for the nostrils and eye.

3 Draw two lines for the neck and a circle for the body.

4 Draw two lines for the tail and add four legs.

you can do it!

Use felt-tips for the lines and add colour with wax crayons. Use different kinds of scribbly crayon marks to add variety.

5 Add kite-shaped plates on its back and spikes at the end of the tail.

Splat-a-fact

Some of the Stegosaurus's back plates were about 2 ft tall (61 cm) and 2 ft (61 cm) wide.

18

Iguanodon

Ig-WAN-oh-don

1 Start with the head.

2 Add the mouth and dots for the eye and nostril.

3 Draw lines for the neck and an oval shape for the body.

4 Draw two lines for the tail.

5 Add two legs, two feet and two arms.

splat-a-fact

The Iguanadon was first found in England.

you can do it!

Use felt-tip for the lines and add colour with watercolour paints. Make a smudged effect by adding green paint to the yellow while it is still wet.

Liopleurodon

Lee-oh-PLOOR-oh-don

1 Cut out the shape of the head.

2 Draw in the eye, nostril and zig-zag mouth.

you can do it!

Cut out the shapes from coloured paper with wax crayon stripes. Stick these on to a sheet of blue paper. Use felt-tip for the lines and white gouache for the air bubbles.

2 Cut out an oval shape for the body and a pointed tail.

3 Cut out four pointed flippers.

MAKE SURE YOU GET AN ADULT TO HELP YOU WHEN USING SCISSORS!

Splat-a-fact

Liopleurodon had strong flippers to speed through water after its prey.

4 Glue all of the body into place and add the head last to overlap.

Styracosaurus

1 Start with the head: add spikes, a horn, an eye and a mouth.

2 Draw a circle for the body.

Splat-a-fact
Styracosaurus means 'spiked lizard'.

3 Draw two curved lines for the tail.

you can do it!
Use felt-tip for the lines and colour in with oil pastels. Smudge colours together with your finger.

4 Add four legs.

25

Velociraptor

Veh-LOSS-er-rap-tor

1 Start with the head and a dot for the eye.

2 Add nostril, mouth and teeth.

3 Draw in two lines for the neck and an oval shape for the body.

4 Draw two lines for the tail and two arms.

you can do it!
Use felt-tip for the lines and add colour usng coloured pencils.

splat-a-fact
Velociraptors starred in the film *Jurassic Park*.

5 Add two legs with clawed feet.

Triceratops

TRY-SERRA-tops

1 Start with the head and a dot for the eye.

2 Draw in horns and the mouth.

3 Draw in an oval shape for the body.

4 Add four legs and draw two curved lines for the tail.

you can do it!

Use a felt-tip pen for the lines. Add colour with watercolour or ink. Use wax crayon then paint on top, the wax will act as a resistant. Make a smudge on the Triceratops by adding orange paint to the pink paint while it is still wet.

splat-a-fact

A Triceratops was almost twice the length of a rhinoceros.

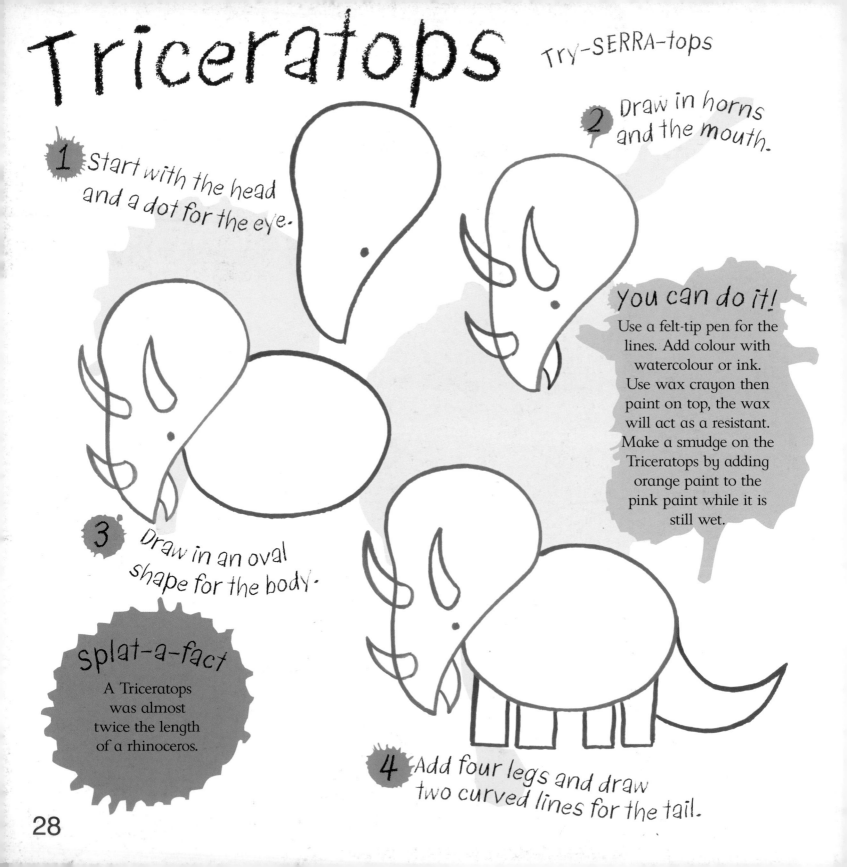

Corythosaurus

core-ith-o-SAW-russ

2 Add a nostril, the mouth, and an egg-shaped bump on top.

3 Draw two lines for the neck joined to a large oval shape.

1 Start with the head and add a dot for the eye.

you can do it!

Use a felt-tip pen for the lines and add colour with watercolour paint. Use purple ink on the yellow body while the paint is still wet.

Draw two curved lines for the tail.

4

splat-a-fact

Corythosaurus had a bony crest on top of its head.

5 Add a curved line to the body and draw two arms and two legs.

30

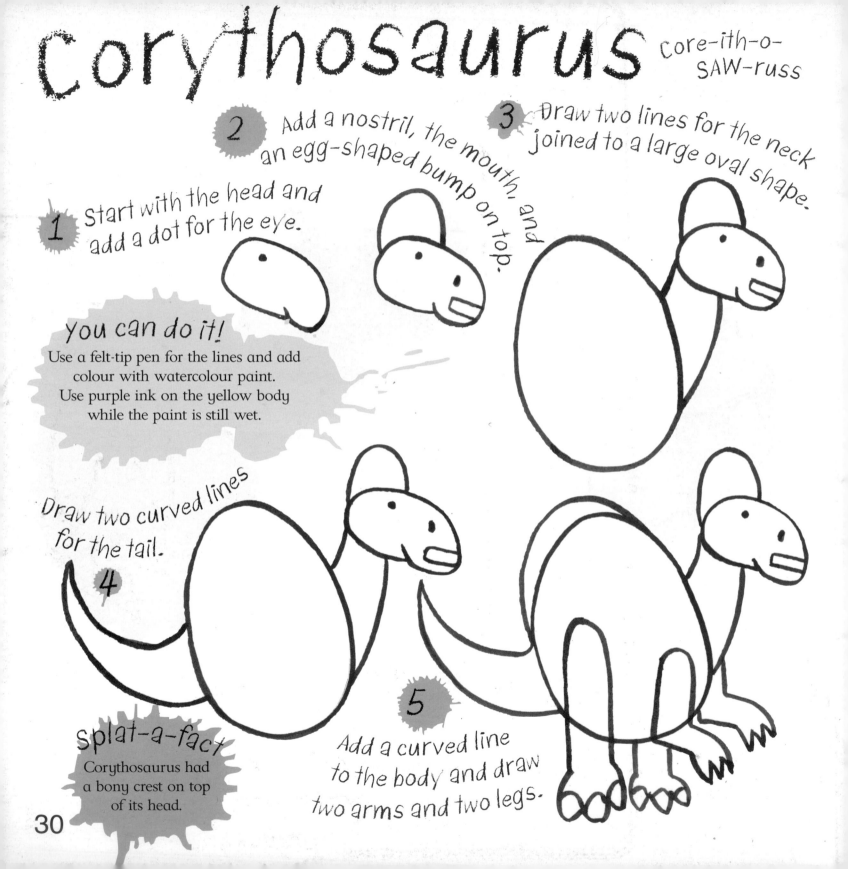

Index

www.salariya.com
where books come to life!

The Salariya Book Company is a UK-based independent publisher of books for children which sells both domestically and internationally. Through our imprints Book House, Scribblers and Scribo we are dedicated to publishing books with real child appeal, using innovative concepts, high-quality illustrations, informative writing and, above all, humour to captivate the minds of young people. With a mind for the environment, all of our books are printed on paper from sustainable forests. Click the links below to visit our imprints' websites, read our Book House Blog or dive into a world of free interactive web books from the best-selling 'You Wouldn't Want To Be...' series.

The Salariya Book Company,
25, Marlborough Place,
Brighton,
East Sussex
BN1 1UB
England
United Kingdom

Tel: 01273 603306
Fax: 01273 621619

rights - anne.murray@salariya.com
press - jamie.pitman@salariya.com
editorial - stephen.haynes@salariya.com
managing director - david@salariya.com

Download our free iPhone and iPad catalogue app. Search for Salariya or Book House

Available on the App Store

Follow us on Facebook and Twitter

www.youtube.com/user/BookHouse100

Children's non-fiction and graphic novels

ScribbIers

Scribo fiction

Fiction for children and teenagers

Bright Start + FREE WEB BOOK!

Free activities, puzzles and web books, with information about our books for babies, toddlers and pre-school

Four free web books

THE BOOK HOUSE BLOG

The Book House blog - competitions, giveaways and current news

FREE WEB BOOKS!